I0011688

Book 1
Python Programming In A Day
BY SAM KEY

&

Book 2
MYSQL Programming
Professional Made Easy
BY SAM KEY

Book 1
Python Programming In A Day
BY SAM KEY

Beginners Power Guide To Learning Python Programming From Scratch

Programming Box Set #36: Python Programming in a Day & MySQL Programming Professional Made Easy

Table Of Contents

Introduction

I want to thank you and congratulate you for purchasing the book, "Python Programming in a Day: Beginners Power Guide To Learning Python Programming From Scratch".

This book contains proven steps and strategies on how you can program using Python in a day or less. It will contain basic information about the programming language. And let you familiarize with programming overall.

Python is one of the easiest and most versatile programming languages today. Also, it is a powerful programming language that is being used by expert developers on their complex computer programs. And its biggest edges against other programming languages are its elegant but simple syntax and readiness for rapid application development.

With python, you can create standalone programs with complex functionalities. In addition, you can combine it or use it as an extension language for programs that were created using other programming languages.

Anyway, this eBook will provide you with easy and understandable tutorial about python. It will only cover the basics of the programming language. On the other hand, the book is a good introduction to some basic concept of programming. It will be not too technical, and it is focused on teaching those who have little knowledge about the craft of developing programs.

By the way, take note that this tutorial will use python 3.4.2. Also, most of the things mentioned here are done in a computer running on Microsoft Windows.

Thanks again for purchasing this book. I hope you enjoy it!

Chapter 1: Getting Prepared

In developing python scripts or programs, you will need a text editor. It is recommended that you use Notepad++. It is a free and open source text editor that you can easily download and install from the internet. For you to have the latest version, go to this link: http://notepad-plus-plus.org/download/v6.6.9.html.

Once you install Notepad++ and you are ready to write python code lines, make sure that you take advantage of its syntax-highlighting feature. To do that, click on Language > P > Python. All python functions will be automatically highlighted when you set the Language to python. It will also highlight strings, numbers, etc. Also, if you save the file for the first time, the save dialog box will automatically set the file to have an extension of .py.

To be able to run your scripts, download and install python into your computer. The latest version, as of this writing, is 3.4.2. You can get python from this link: https://www.python.org/download.

And to be able to test run your python scripts in Notepad++, go to Run > Run... or press the F5 key. A small dialogue box will appear, and it will require you to provide the path for the compiler or a program that will execute your script. In this case, you will need to direct Notepad++ to the python executable located in the installation folder.

By default or if you did not change the installation path of python, it can be found on the root folder on the drive where your operating system is installed. If your operating system is on drive C of your computer, the python executable can be found on C:\Python34\python.exe. Paste that line on the dialogue box and add the following line: $(FULL_CURRENT_PATH). Separate the location of the python.exe and the line with a space, and enclosed the latter in double quotes. It should look like this:

C:\Python34\python.exe "$(FULL_CURRENT_PATH)"

Save this setting by pressing the Save button in the dialogue box. Another window will popup. It will ask you to name the setting and assign a shortcut key to it. Just name it python34 and set the shortcut key to F9. Press the OK button and close the dialogue box. With that setting, you can test run your program by just pressing the F9 key.

By the way, if the location you have set is wrong, the python executable will not run. So to make sure you got it right, go to python folder. And since you are already there, copy python.exe, and paste its shortcut on your desktop. You will need to access it later.

And you are all set. You can proceed on learning python now.

Chapter 2: Interactive Mode – Mathematical Operations

Before you develop multiple lines of code for a program, it will be best for you to start playing around with Python's interactive mode first. The interactive mode allows a developer to see immediate results of what he will code in his program. For new python users, it can help them familiarize themselves on python's basic functions, commands, and syntax.

To access the interactive mode, just open python.exe. If you followed the instructions in the previous chapter, its shortcut should be already on your desktop. Just open it and the python console will appear.

Once you open the python executable, a command console like window will appear. It will greet you with a short message that will tell you the version of python that you are using and some command that can provide you with various information about python. At the bottom of the message, you will the primary prompt (>>>). Beside that is the blinking cursor. In there, you can just type the functions or commands you want to use or execute. For starters, type credits and press Enter.

Mathematical Operations in Interactive Mode

You can actually use the interactive mode as a calculator. Try typing 1 + 1 and press Enter. Immediately after you press the Enter, the console provided you with the answer to the equation 1 + 1. And then it created a new line and the primary prompt is back.

In python, there are eight basic mathematical operations that you can execute. And they are:

- Addition = 1 + 1

- Subtraction = 1 – 1

- Multiplication = 1 * 1

- Division = 1 / 1

  In older versions of Python, if you divide integers and the division will result to a decimal, Python will only return an integer. For example, if you divide 3 by 2, you will get 1 as an answer. And if you divide 20 by 39, you will get a zero. Also, take note that the result is not rounded off. Python will just truncate all numbers after the decimal point.

  In case you want to get an accurate quotient with decimals, you must convert the integers into floating numbers. To do that, you can simply add a decimal point after the numbers.

- Floor Division = 1 // 1

  If you are dividing floating numbers and you just want to get the integer quotient or you do not want the decimals to be included, you can perform floor division instead. For example, floor dividing 5.1515 by 2.0 will give you a 2 as an integer quotient.

- Modulo = 1 % 1

  The modulo operator will allow you to get the remainder from a division from two numbers. For example, typing 5 % 2 will give you a result of 1 since 5 divided by two is 2 remainder 1.

- Negation = -1

  Adding a hyphen before a number will make it a negative number. You can perform double, triple, or multiple negations with this operator. For example, typing -23 will result into -23. Typing --23 will result into 23. Typing -----23 will result into -23.

- Absolute Value = abs(1)

When this is used to a number, the number will be converted to its absolute value or will be always positive. For example, abs (-41) will return 41.

Python calculates equation using the PEMDAS order, the order of operations that are taught in Basic Math, Geometry, and Algebra subjects in schools. By the way, PEMDAS stands for Parentheses, Exponents, Multiplication, Division, Addition, and Subtraction.

Chapter 3: Interactive Mode – Variables

During your Math subject when you were in grade or high school, your teacher might have taught you about variables. In Math, variables are letters that serve as containers for numbers of known and unknown value. In Python or any programming language, variables are important. They act as storage of values. And their presence makes the lives of developers easy.

However, unlike in school, variables in programming languages are flexible when it comes to their names and functions. In Python, variables can have names instead of a single letter. Also, they can also contain or represent text or strings.

Assigning Values to Variables

Assigning a value to a variable is easy in Python. You can just type the name of your variable, place an equal sign afterwards, and place the value you want to be contained or stored in the variable. For example:

```
>>> x = 151
```

When you assign a value in a variable, Python will not reply any message. Instead, it will just put your cursor on the next primary prompt. In the example, you have assigned the value 151 to the variable x. To check if it worked, type x on the console and press Enter. Python will respond with the value of the variable x.

Just like numbers, you can perform arithmetical operations with variable. For example, try typing x – 100 in the console and press Enter. Python will calculate the equation, and return the number 51 since 151 – 100 = 51. And of course, you can perform mathematical operations with multiple variables in one line.

By the way, in case that you did not define or assign a value to a new variable, Python will return an error if you use it. For example, if you try to subtract x with y, you will get an error that will say name 'y' is not defined. You received that message since you have not assigned anything to the variable y yet.

Programming Box Set #36: Python Programming in a Day & MySQL Programming Professional Made Easy

In addition, you can assign and change the value of a variable anytime. Also, the variable's value will not change if you do not assign anything to it. The variable and its value will stay in your program as long as you do not destroy it, delete it, or close the program.

To delete a variable, type del then the name of the variable. For example:

>>> del x

Once you try to access the variable again by typing its name and pressing Enter after you delete it, Python will return an error message saying that the variable is not defined.

Also, you can assign calculated values to a variable. For example:

>>> z = 1 + 4

If you type that, type z, and press Enter, Python will reply with 5. Variables are that easy to manipulate in Python.

You can also assign the value of one variable to another. Below is an example:

>>> y = 2

>>> z = y

The variable z's value will be changed to 2.

Chapter 4: Interactive Mode – Strings

Your program will not be all about numbers. Of course, you would want to add some text into it. In Python, you can do that by using strings. A string or string literal is a series of alphanumeric numbers or characters. A string can be a word or sentence. A lone character can be also considered as a string. To make your program display a string, you will need to use the print function. Below is an example on how to use it:

```
>>> print ( "Dogs are cute." )
```

To display a string using the print function properly, you will need to enclose the string with parentheses and double quotations. Without the parentheses, you will receive a syntax error. Without the quotes, Python will think that you are trying to make it display a variable's value.

By the way, in older versions of Python, you can use print without the parentheses. However, in version 3 and newer, print was changed to as a function. Because of that, it will require parentheses.

For example:

```
>>> print ( "Dogs" )
```

That line will make Python print the word or string Dogs. On the other hand:

```
>>> print ( Dogs )
```

That line will return a variable not defined error. With that being said, you can actually print or display the content of a variable. For example:

>>> x = 14

>>> print (x)

The print function will display the number 14 on the screen. By the way, you can also use single quotes or even triple single or double quotes. However, it is recommendable to use a single double for those who are just started in program development.

Assigning Strings to Variables

Assigning strings to variables is easy. And it is the same as assigning numbers to them. The only difference is that you will need to enclose the string value in double quotations or reverse commas as some developers call them. For example:

>>> stringvariable = "This is a string."

If you type stringvariable in the interactive mode console, it will display the This is a string text. On the other hand, if you do this:

>>> print (stringvariable)

Python will print the string, too.

Strings can include punctuation and symbols. However, there are some symbols or punctuations that can mess up your assignment and give you a syntax error. For example:

>>> samplestring = "And he said, "Hi.""

In this case, you will get a syntax error because the appearance of another double quote has appeared before the double quote that should be enclosing the string. Unfortunately, Python cannot recognize what you are trying to do here. Because of that, you need the by escaping the string literal.

To escape, you must place the escape character backslash (\) before the character that might produce conflict. In the example's case, the characters that might produce a syntax error are the two double quotes inside. Below is the fixed version of the previous paragraph:

>>> samplestring = "And he said, \"Hi.\""

Writing the string assignment like that will not produce an error. In case you print or type and enter the variable samplestring in the console, you will see the string that you want to appear, which is And he said, "Hi.".

Escape Sequences in Python

Not all characters are needed to be escaped. Due to that, the characters that you can escape or the number of escape sequences are limited. Also, escape sequences are not only for preventing syntax errors. They are also used to add special characters such as new line and carriage return to your strings. Below is a list of the escape sequences you can use in Python:

- \\ = Backslash (\)

- \" = Double quote (")

- \' = Single quote (')

- \b = Backspace

- \a = ASCII Bell

- \n = Linefeed

- \f = Formfeed

- \t = Horizontal Tab

- \r = Carriage Return

- \v = ASCII Vertical Tab

Preventing Escape Sequences to Work

There will be times that the string that you want to print or use might accidentally contain an escape sequence. Though, it is a bit rare since the backslash character is seldom used in everyday text. Nevertheless, it is still best that you know how to prevent it. Below is an example of an escape sequence that might produce undesirable results to your program:

>>> print ("C:\Windows\notepad.exe")

When Python processes that, you might encounter a problem when you use since the \n in the middle of the string will break the string. For you to visualize it better, below is the result:

>>> print ("C:\Windows\notepad.exe")

C:\Windows

otepad.exe

>>> _

To prevent that you must convert your string to a raw string. You can do that by placing the letter r before the string that you will print. Below is an example:

```
>>> print ( r"C:\Windows\notepad.exe" )
C:\Windows\notepad.exe
>>> _
```

Basic String Operations

In Python, you can perform operations on your strings. These basic string operations also use the common arithmetical operators, but when those operators are used on strings, they will produce different results. There are two of these. And they use the + and * operators. Below are examples on how to use them:

```
>>> print ( "cat" + "dog" )
catdog
>>> print ( "cat" * 3 )
catcatcat
>>> _
```

When the + operator is used between two strings, it will combine them. On the other hand, if the multiplication operator is used, the string will be repeated depending on the number indicated.

By the way, you cannot use operators between strings and numbers – with the exception of the multiplication symbol. For example:

>>> variable_x = 1 + "text"

The example above will return an unsupported operand type since Python does not know what to do when you add a string and a number.

Chapter 5: Transition from Interactive Mode to Programming Mode

Alright, by this time, you must already have a good feel on Python's interactive mode. You also know the basic concepts of variables, strings, and numbers. Now, it is time to put them together and create a simple program.

You can now close Python's window and open Notepad++. A new file should be currently opened once you open that program. The next step is to set the Language setting into Python. And save the file. Any name will do as long that you make sure that your file's extension is set to .py or Python file. In case the save function does not work, type anything on the text file. After you save it, remove the text you typed.

Now, you will start getting used to programming mode. Programming mode is where program development start. Unlike interactive mode, programming mode requires you to code first, save your file, and run it on Python. To get a feel of the programming mode, copy this sample below:

```
print ( "Hello World!" )

print ( "This is a simple program that aims to display text." )

print ( "That is all." )

input ( "Press Enter Key to End this Program" )
```

If you followed the instructions on the Getting Prepared chapter, press the F9 key. Once you do, Python will run and execute your script. It will be read line by line by Python just like in Interactive mode. The only difference is that the primary prompt is not there, and you cannot input any command while it is running.

Input Function

On the other hand, the example code uses the input function. The input function's purpose is to retrieve any text that the user will type in the program and wait for the Enter key to be pressed before going to the next line of code below it. And when the user presses the key the program will close since there are no remaining lines of code to execute.

By the way, if you remove the input function from the example, the program will just print the messages in it and close itself. And since Python will process those lines within split seconds, you will be unable to see if it work. So, in the following examples and lessons, the input function will be used to temporarily pause your scripts or prevent your program to close prematurely.

You can use the input function to assign values to variables. Check this example out:

```
print ( "Can you tell me your name?" )

name = input("Please type your name: ")

print ( "Your name is " + name + ".")

print ( "That is all." )

input ( "Press Enter Key to End this Program. \n" )
```

In this example, the variable name was assigned a value that will come from user input through the input function. When you run it, the program will pause on the Please type your name part and wait for user input. The user can place almost anything on it. And when he presses enter, Python will capture the text, and store it to variable name.

Once the name is established, the print function will confirm it and mention the content of the name variable.

Data Type Conversion

You can also use the input function to get numbers. However, to make sure the program will understand that its numbers that it will receive, make sure that your input does not include non-numeric characters. Below is a sample code of an adding program:

```
print ( "This program will add two numbers you would input." )

first_number = input ( "Type the first number: " )

second_number = input ( "Type the second number: " )

sum = int(first_number) + int(second_number)

print ( "The sum is " + str(sum) )

input ( "Press Enter Key to End this Program. \n" )
```

In this example, the program tries to get numbers from the user. And get the sum of those two numbers. However, there is a problem. The input function only produces string data. That means that even if you type in a number, the input will still assign a string version of that number to the variable.

And since they are both strings, you cannot add them as numbers. And if you do add them, it will result into a joined string. For example, if the first number was 1 and the second number was 2, the sum that will appear will be 12, which is mathematically wrong.

In order to fix that, you will need to convert the strings into its numeric form. In this example, they will be converted to integers. With the help of the int function, that can be easily done. Any variable will be converted to integer when placed inside the int function.

So, to get the integer sum of the first_number and second_number, both of them were converted into integers. By the way, converting only one of them will result into an error. With that done, the sum of the two numbers will be correctly produced, which 3.

21

Now the second roadblock is the print function. In the last print function, the example used an addition operator to join the The sum is text and the variable sum. However, since the variable sum is an integer, the operation will return an error. Just like before, you should convert the variable in order for the operation to work. In this case, the sum variable was converted to a string using the str function.

There are other data types in Python – just like with other programming languages. This part will not cover the technicalities of those data types and about the memory allocation given to them, but this part is to just familiarize you with it. Nevertheless, below is a list of a few of the data type conversion functions you might use while programming in Python:

- Long() – converts data to a long integer

- Hex() – converts integers to hexadecimal

- Float() – converts data to floating-point

- Unichr() – converts integers to Unicode

- Chr() – converts integers to characters

- Oct() – converts integers to octal

Chapter 6: Programming Mode – Conditional Statements

Just displaying text and getting text from user are not enough for you to make a decent program out of Python. You need your program to be capable of interacting with your user and be capable of producing results according to their inputs.

Because of that, you will need to use conditional statements. Conditional statements allow your program to execute code blocks according to the conditions you set. For you to get more familiar with conditional statements, check the example below:

```
print ( "Welcome to Guess the Number Game! " )

magic_number = input ( "Type your guess: " )

if ( magic_number  == "1" ):

    print ( "You Win!" )

else:

    print ( "You Lose!" )

input ( "Press enter to exit this program " )
```

In this example, the if or conditional statement is used. The syntax of this function differs a bit from the other functions discussed earlier. In this one, you will need to set a conditional argument on its parentheses. The condition is that if the variable magic_number is equal to 1, then the code block under it will run. The colon after the condition indicates that it will have a code block beneath it.

When you go insert a code block under a statement, you will need to indent them. The code block under the if statement is print ("You Win!"). Because of that, it is and should be indented. If the condition is satisfied, which will happen if the user entered 1, then the code block under if will run. If the condition was not satisfied, it will be ignored, and Python will parse on the next line with the same indent level as if.

That next line will be the else statement. If and else go hand in hand. The have identical function. If their conditions are satisfied, then the program will run the code block underneath them. However, unlike if, else has a preset condition. Its condition is that whenever the previous conditional statement is not satisfied, then it will run its code block. And that also means that if the previous conditional statement's condition was satisfied, it will not run.

Due to that, if the user guesses the right magic number, then the code block of if will run and the else statement's code block will be ignored. If the user was unable to guess the right magic number, if's code block will be ignored and else's code block will run.

Conclusion

Thank you again for purchasing this book!

I hope this book was able to help you to understand the basic concepts of programming and become familiar in Python in just one day.

The next step is to research and learn looping in Python. Loops are control structures that can allow your program to repeat various code blocks. They are very similar to conditional statements. The only difference is that, their primary function is to repeat all the lines of codes placed inside their codeblocks. Also, whenever the parser of Python reaches the end of its code block, it will go back to the loop statement and see if the condition is still satisfied. In case that it is, it will loop again. In case that it does not, it will skip its code block and move to the next line with the same indent level.

In programming, loops are essential. Truth be told, loops compose most functionalities of complex programs. Also, when it comes to coding efficiency, loops makes program shorter and faster to develop. Using loops in your programs will reduce the size of your codes. And it will reduce the amount of time you need to write all the codes you need to achieve the function you desire in your program.

If you do not use loops in your programs, you will need to repeat typing or pasting lines of codes that might span to hundreds of instances – whereas if you use loops in your programs, those hundred instances can be reduced into five or seven lines of codes.

There are multiple methods on how you can create a loop in your program. Each loop method or function has their unique purposes. Trying to imitate another loop method with one loop method can be painstaking.

On the other hand, once you are done with loops, you will need to upgrade your current basic knowledge about Python. Research about all the other operators that were not mentioned in this book, the other data types and their quirks and functions, simple statements, compound statements, and top-level components.

To be honest, Python is huge. You have just seen a small part of it. And once you delve deeper on its other capabilities and the possible things you could create with it, you will surely get addicted to programming.

Finally, if you enjoyed this book, please take the time to share your thoughts and post a review on Amazon. We do our best to reach out to readers and provide the best value we can. Your positive review will help us achieve that. It'd be greatly appreciated!

Thank you and good luck!

Book 2
MYSQL Programming
Professional Made Easy

By Sam Key

Expert MYSQL Programming Language Success in a Day for any Computer User!

Programming Box Set #36: Python Programming in a Day & MySQL Programming Professional Made Easy

Table Of Contents

Introduction

I want to thank you and congratulate you for purchasing the book, "MYSQL Programming Professional Made Easy: Expert MYSQL Programming Language Success in a Day for any Computer User!".

This book contains proven steps and strategies on how to manage MySQL databases.

The book will teach you the fundamentals of SQL and how to apply it on MySQL. It will cover the basic operations such as creating and deleting tables and databases. Also, it will tell you how to insert, update, and delete records in MySQL. In the last part of the book, you will be taught on how to connect to your MySQL server and send queries to your database using PHP.

Thankfully, by this time, this subject is probably a piece of cake for you since you might already have experienced coding in JavaScript and PHP, which are prerequisites to learning MySQL.

However, it does not mean that you will have a difficult time learning MySQL if you do not have any idea on those two scripting languages. In this book, you will learn about SQL, which works a bit different from programming languages.

Being knowledgeable alone with SQL can give you a solid idea on how MySQL and other RDBMS work. Anyway, thanks again for purchasing this book, I hope you enjoy it!

Chapter 1: Introduction to MySQL

This book will assume that you are already knowledgeable about PHP. It will focus on database application on the web. The examples here will use PHP as the main language to use to access a MySQL database. Also, this will be focused on Windows operating system users.

As of now, MySQL is the most popular database system by PHP programmers. Also, it is the most popular database system on the web. A few of the websites that use MySQL to store their data are Facebook, Wikipedia, and Twitter.

Commonly, MySQL databases are ran on web servers. Because of that, you need to use a server side scripting language to use it.

A few of the good points of MySQL against other database systems are it is scalable (it is good to use in small or large scale applications), fast, easy to use, and reliable. Also, if you are already familiar with SQL, you will not have any problems in manipulating MySQL databases.

Preparation

In the first part of this book, you will learn SQL or Standard Query Language. If you have a database program, such as Microsoft Access, installed in your computer, you can use it to practice and apply the statements you will learn.

In case you do not, you have two options. Your first option is to get a hosting account package that includes MySQL and PHP. If you do not want to spend tens of dollars for a paid web hosting account, you can opt for a free one. However, be informed that most of them will impose limitations or add annoyances, such as ads, in your account. Also, some of them have restrictions that will result to your account being banned once you break one of them.

Your second option is to get XAMMP, a web server solution that includes Apache, MySQL, and PHP. It will turn your computer into a local web server. And with it, you can play around with your MySQL database and the PHP codes you want to experiment with. Also, it comes with phpMyAdmin. A tool that will be discussed later in this book.

Chapter 2: Database and SQL

What is a database? A database is an application or a file wherein you can store data. It is used and included in almost all types of computer programs. A database is usually present in the background whether the program is a game, a word processor, or a website.

A database can be a storage location for a player's progress and setting on a game. It can be a storage location for dictionaries and preferences in word processors. And it can be a storage location for user accounts and page content in websites.

There are different types and forms of databases. A spreadsheet can be considered a database. Even a list of items in a text file can be considered one, too. However, unlike the database that most people know or familiar with, those kinds of databases are ideal for small applications.

RDBMS

The type of database that is commonly used for bigger applications is RDBMS or relational database management system. MySQL is an RDBMS. Other RDBMS that you might have heard about are Oracle database, Microsoft Access, and SQL Server.

Inside an RDBMS, there are tables that are composed of rows, columns, and indexes. Those tables are like spreadsheets. Each cell in a table holds a piece of data. Below is an example table:

id	username	password	email	firstname	lastname
1	Johnnyxxx	123abc	jjxxx@gmail.com	Johnny	Stew
2	cutiepatutie	qwertyuiop	cuteme@yahoo.com	Sara	Britch
3	mastermiller	theGear12	mgshades@gmail.com	Master	Miller
4	j_sasaki	H9fmaNCa	j_sasaki@gmail.com	Johnny	Sasaki

Note: this same table will be used as the main reference of all the examples in this book. Also, developers usually encrypt their passwords in their databases. They are not encrypted for the sake of an example.

In the table, which the book will refer to as the account table under the sample database, there are six columns (or fields) and they are id, username, password, email, firstname, and lastname. As of now, there are only four rows. Rows can be also called entries or records. Take note that the first row is not part of the count. They are just there to represent the name of the columns as headers.

An RDBMS table can contain one or more tables.

Compared to other types of databases, RDBMS are easier to use and manage because it comes with a standardized set of method when it comes to accessing and manipulating data. And that is SQL or Standard Query Language.

SQL

Before you start learning MySQL, you must familiarize yourself with SQL or Standard Query Language first. SQL is a language used to manipulate and access relational database management systems. It is not that complicated compared to learning programming languages.

Few of the things you can do with databases using SQL are:

- Get, add, update, and delete data from databases
- Create, modify, and delete databases
- Modify access permissions in databases

Most database programs use SQL as the standard method of accessing databases, but expect that some of them have a bit of variations. Some statements have different names or keywords while some have different methods to do things. Nevertheless, most of the usual operations are the same for most of them.

A few of the RDBMS that you can access using SQL – with little alterations – are MySQL, SQL Server, and Microsoft Access.

Chapter 3: SQL Syntax

SQL is like a programming language. It has its own set of keywords and syntax rules. Using SQL is like talking to the database. With SQL, you can pass on commands to the database in order for it to present and manipulate the data it contains for you. And you can do that by passing queries and statements to it.

SQL is commonly used interactively in databases. As soon as you send a query or statement, the database will process it immediately. You can perform some programming in SQL, too. However, it is much easier to leave the programming part to other programming languages. In the case of MySQL, it is typical that most of the programming is done with PHP, which is the most preferred language to use with it.

SQL's syntax is simple. Below is an example:

SELECT username FROM account

In the example, the query is commanding the database to get all the data under the username column from the account table. The database will reply with a recordset or a collection of records.

In MySQL, databases will also return the number of rows it fetched and the duration that it took to fetch the result.

Case Sensitivity

As you can see, the SQL query is straightforward and easy to understand. Also, take note that unlike PHP, MySQL is not case sensitive. Even if you change the keyword SELECT's case to select, it will still work. For example:

seLeCT username from account

However, as a standard practice, it is best that you type keywords on uppercase and values in lowercase.

Line Termination

In case that you will perform or send consecutive queries or a multiline query, you need to place a semicolon at the end of each statement to separate them. By the way, MySQL does not consider a line to be a statement when it sees a new line character – meaning, you can place other parts of your queries on multiple lines. For example:

SELECT

username

FROM

account;

New lines are treated like a typical whitespace (spaces and tabs) character. And the only accepted line terminator is a semicolon. In some cases, semicolons are not needed to terminate a line.

Chapter 4: SQL Keywords and Statements

When you memorize the SQL keywords, you can say that you are already know SQL or MySQL. Truth be told, you will be mostly using only a few SQL keywords for typical database management. And almost half of the queries you will be making will be SELECT queries since retrieving data is always the most used operation in databases.

Before you learn that, you must know how to create a database first.

CREATE DATABASE

Creating a database is simple. Follow the syntax below:

CREATE DATABASE <name of database>;

To create the sample database where the account table is located, this is all you need to type:

CREATE DATABASE sample;

Easy, right? However, an empty database is a useless database. You cannot enter any data to it yet since you do not have tables yet.

CREATE TABLE

Creating a table requires a bit of planning. Before you create a table, you must already know the columns you want to include in it. Also, you need to know the size, type, and other attributes of the pieces of data that you will insert on your columns. Once you do, follow the syntax below:

CREATE TABLE <name of table>

(

<name of column 1> <data type(size)> <attributes>,

<name of column 2> <data type(size)> <attributes>,

<name of column 3> <data type(size)> <attributes>

);

By the way, you cannot just create a table out of nowhere. To make sure that the table you will create will be inside a database, you must be connected to one. Connection to databases will be discussed in the later part of this book. As of now, imagine that you are now connected to the sample database that was just created in the previous section.

To create the sample account table, you need to do this:

CREATE TABLE account

(

id int(6) PRIMARY KEY UNSIGNED AUTO_INCREMENT PRIMARY KEY,

username varchar(16),

password varchar(16),

email varchar(32),

firstname var(16),

lastname var(16),

);

The example above commands the database to create a table named account. Inside the parentheses, the columns that will be created inside the account table are specified. They are separated with a comma. The first column that was created was the id column.

According to the example, the database needs to create the id column (id). It specified that the type of data that it will contain would be integers with six characters (int(6)). Also, it specified some optional attributes. It said that the id column will be the PRIMARY KEY of the table and its values will AUTO_INCREMENT – these will be discussed later. Also, it specified that the integers or data under it will be UNSIGNED, which means that only positive integers will be accepted.

MySQL Data Types

As mentioned before, databases or RDBMS accept multiple types of data. To make databases clean, it is required that you state the data type that you will input in your table's columns. Aside from that, an RDBMS also needs to know the size of the data that you will enter since it will need to allocate the space it needs to store the data you will put in it. Providing precise information about the size of your data will make your database run optimally.

Below are some of the data types that you will and can store in a MySQL database:

- INT(size) – integer data type. Numbers without fractional components or decimal places. A column with an INT data type can accept any number between -2147483648 to 2147483648. In case that you specified that it will be UNSIGNED, the column will accept any number between 0 to 4294967295. You can specify the number of digits with INT. The maximum is 11 digits – it will include the negative sign (-).
- FLOAT(size, decimal) – float data type. Numbers with fractional components or decimal places. It cannot be UNSIGNED. You can specify the number of digits it can handle and the number of decimal places it will store. If you did not specify the size and number of decimals, MySQL will set it to 10 digits and 2 decimal places (the decimal places is included in the count of the digits). Float can have the maximum of 24 digits.
- TIME – time will be stored and formatted as HH:MM:SS.
- DATE – date will be stored and formatted as YYYY-MM-DD. It will not accept any date before year 1,000. And it will not accept date that exceeds 31 days and 12 months.
- DATETIME – combination of DATE and TIME formatted as YYYY-MM-DD HH:MM:SS.
- TIMESTAMP – formatted differently from DATETIME. Its format is YYYYMMDDHHMMSS. It can only store date and time between 19700101000000 and 20371231235959 (not accurate).
- CHAR(size) – stores strings with fixed size. It can have a size of 1 to 255 characters. It uses static memory allocation, which makes it perform faster than VARCHAR. It performs faster because the database will just multiply its way to reach the location of the data you want instead of searching every byte to find the data that you need. To make the data fixed length, it is padded with spaces after the last character.
- VARCHAR(size) – stores strings with variable length size. It can have a size of 1 to 255 characters. It uses dynamic memory allocation, which is slower than static. However, when using VARCHAR, it is mandatory to specify the data's size.
- BLOB –store BLOBs (Binary Large Objects). Data is stored as byte strings instead of character strings (in contrast to TEXT). This makes it possible to store images, documents, or other files in the database.
- TEXT – store text with a length of 65535 characters or less.
- ENUM(x, y, z) – with this, you can specify the values that can be only stored.

INT, BLOB, and TEXT data types can be set smaller or bigger. For example, you can use TINYINT instead of INT to store smaller data. TINYINT can only hold values ranging from -128 to 127 compared to INT that holds values ranging from -2147483648 to 2147483647.

The size of the data type ranges from TINY, SMALL, MEDIUM, NORMAL, and BIG.

- TINYINT, SMALLINT, MEDIUMINT, INT, and BIGINT
- TINYBLOB, SMALLBLOB, MEDIUMBLOB, BLOB, and BIGBLOB
- TINYTEXT, SMALLTEXT, MEDIUMTEXT, TEXT, and BIGTEXT

You already know how to create databases and tables. Now, you need to learn how to insert values inside those tables.

INSERT INTO and VALUES

There are two ways to insert values in your database. Below is the syntax for the first method:

INSERT INTO <name of table>

VALUES (<value 1>, <value 2>, <value 3>);

The same result be done by:

INSERT INTO <name of table>

(<column 1>, <column 2>, <column 3>)

VALUES (<value 1>, <value 2>, <value 3>);

Take note that the first method will assign values according to the arrangement of your columns in the tables. In case you do not want to enter a data to one of the columns in your table, you will be forced to enter an empty value.

On the other hand, if you want full control of the INSERT operation, it will be much better to indicate the name of the corresponding columns that will be given data. Take note that the database will assign the values you will write with respect of the arrangement of the columns in your query.

For example, if you want to insert data in the example account table, you need to do this:

INSERT INTO account

(username, password, email, firstname, lastname)

VALUES

("Johnnyxxx", "123abc", "jjxxx@gmail.com, "Johnny", "Stew");

The statement will INSERT one entry to the database. You might have noticed that the example did not include a value for the ID field. You do not need to do that since the ID field has the AUTO_INCREMENT attribute. The database will be the one to generate a value to it.

SELECT and FROM

To check if the entry you sent was saved to the database, you can use SELECT. As mentioned before, the SELECT statement will retrieve all the data that you want from the database. Its syntax is:

SELECT <column 1> FROM <name of table>;

If you use this in the example account table and you want to get all the usernames in it, you can do it by:

SELECT username FROM account;

In case that you want to multiple records from two or more fields, you can do that by specifying another column. For example:

SELECT username, email FROM account;

WHERE

Unfortunately, using SELECT alone will provide you with tons of data. And you do not want that all the time. To filter out the results you want or to specify the data you want to receive, you can use the WHERE clause. For example:

SELECT <column 1> FROM <name of table>

WHERE <column> <operator> <value>;

If ever you need to get the username of all the people who have Johnny as their first name in the account table, you do that by:

SELECT username FROM account

WHERE firstname = "Johnny";

In the query above, the database will search all the records in the username column that has the value Johnny on the firstname column. The query will return Johnnyxxx and j_sasaki.

LIMIT

What if you only need a specific number of records to be returned? You can use the LIMIT clause for that. For example:

SELECT <column 1> FROM <name of table>

LIMIT <number>;

If you only want one record from the email column to be returned when you use SELECT on the account table, you can do it by:

SELECT email FROM account

LIMIT 1;

You can the LIMIT clause together with the WHERE clause for you to have a more defined search. For example:

SELECT username FROM account

WHERE firstname = "Johnny"

LIMIT 1;

Instead of returning two usernames that have Johnny in the firstname field, it will only return one.

UPDATE and SET

What if you made a mistake and you want to append an entry on your table? Well, you can use UPDATE for that. For example:

UPDATE <name of table>

SET <column 1>=<value 1>, <column 1>=<value 1>, <column 1>=<value 1>

WHERE <column> <operator> <value>;

In the example account table, if you want to change the name of all the people named Master to a different one, you can do that by:

UPDATE account

SET firstname="David"

WHERE firstname="Master";

Take note, you can perform an UPDATE without the WHERE clause. However, doing so will make the database think that you want to UPDATE all the records in the table. Remember that it is a bit complex to ROLLBACK changes in MySQL, so be careful.

DELETE

If you do not to remove an entire row, you can use DELETE. However, if you just want to delete or remove one piece of data in a column, it is better to use UPDATE and place a blank value instead. To perform a DELETE, follow this syntax:

DELETE FROM <name of table>

WHERE <column> <operator> <value>;

If you want to delete the first row in the account table, do this:

DELETE FROM account

WHERE id = 1;

Just like with the UPDATE statement, make sure that you use the WHERE clause when using DELETE. If not, all the rows in your table will disappear.

TRUNCATE TABLE

If you just want to remove all the data inside your table and keep all the settings that you have made to it you need to use TRUNCATE TABLE. This is the syntax for it:

TRUNCATE TABLE <name of table>;

If you want to do that to the account table, do this by entering:

TRUNCATE TABLE account;

DROP TABLE and DROP DATABASE

Finally, if you want to remove a table or database, you can use DROP. Below are examples on how to DROP the account table and sample database.

DROP TABLE account;

DROP DATABASE sample;

Chapter 5: MySQL and PHP

You already know how to manage a MySQL server to the most basic level. Now, it is time to use all those statements and use PHP to communicate with the MySQL server.

To interact or access a MySQL database, you need to send SQL queries to it. There are multiple ways you can do that. But if you want to do it in the web or your website, you will need to use a server side scripting language. And the best one to use is PHP.

In PHP, you can communicate to a MySQL server by using PDO (PHP Data Objects), MySQL extension, or MySQLi extension. Compared to MySQLi extension, PDO is a better choice when communicating with a MySQL database. However, in this book, only MySQLi extension will be discussed since it is less complex and easier to use.

Connecting to a MySQL database:

Before you can do or say anything to a MySQL server or a database, you will need to connect to it first. To do that, follow this example:

```
<?php
$dbservername = "localhost";
$dbusername = "YourDataBaseUserName";
$dbpassword = "YourPassword12345";

// Create a new connection object
$dbconnection = new mysqli($dbservername, $ dbusername, $ dbpassword);

// Check if connection was successful
if ($dbconnection->connect_error) {
    die("Connection failed/error: " . $dbconnection->connect_error);
}
echo "Connected successfully to database";
?>
```

In this example, you are using PHP's MySQLi to connect to your database. If you are going to test the code in the server that you installed in your computer, use localhost for your database's server name.

By the way, to prevent hackers on any random internet surfers to edit or access your databases, your MySQL server will require you to set a username and password. Every time you connect to it, you will need to include it to the parameters of the mysqli object.

In the example, you have created an object under the mysqli class. All the information that the server will send to you will be accessible in this object.

The third block of code is used to check if your connection request encountered any trouble. As you can see, the if statement is checking whether the connect_error property of the object $dbconnection contains a value. If it does, the code will be terminated and return an error message.

On the other hand, if the connect_error is null, the code will proceed and echo a message that will tell the user that the connection was successful.

Closing a connection
To close a mysqli object's connection, just invoke its close() method. For example:

$dbconnection->close();

Creating a new MySQL Database
```
<?php
$dbservername = "localhost";
$dbusername = "YourDataBaseUserName";
$dbpassword = "YourPassword12345";

// Create a new connection object
$dbconnection = new mysqli($dbservername, $ dbusername, $ dbpassword);

// Check if connection was successful
if ($dbconnection->connect_error) {
    die("Connection failed/error: " . $dbconnection->connect_error);
}


// Creating a Database

$dbSQL = "CREATE DATABASE YourDatabaseName";

if ($dbconnection->query($dbSQL) === TRUE) {

        echo "YourDatabaseName was created.";

}

else {

        echo "An error was encountered while creating your database: " .
$dbconnection->error;
```

```
}

$dbconnection->close();
?>
```

Before you request a database to be created, you must connect to your MySQL server first. Once you establish a connection, you will need to tell your server to create a database by sending an SQL query.

The $dbSQL variable was created to hold the query string that you will send. You do not need to do this, but creating a variable for your queries is good practice since it will make your code more readable. If you did not create a variable holder for your SQL, you can still create a database by:

```
$dbconnection->query("CREATE DATABASE YourDatabaseName")
```

The if statement was used to both execute the query method of $dbconnection and to check if your server will be able to do it. If it does, it will return a value of TRUE. The if statement will inform you that you were able to create your database.

On the other hand, if it returns false or an error instead, the example code will return a message together with the error.

Once the database was created, the connection was closed.

Interacting with a Database

Once you create a database, you can now send SQL queries and do some operations in it. Before you do that, you need to connect to the server and then specify the name of the database, which you want to interact with, in the parameters of the mysqli class when creating a mysqli object. For example:

```php
<?php
$dbservername = "localhost";
$dbusername = "YourDataBaseUserName";
$dbpassword = "YourPassword12345";

$dbname = "sample"

// Create a new connection object
$dbconnection = new mysqli($dbservername, $ dbusername, $ dbpassword, $sample);

// Check if connection was successful
if ($dbconnection->connect_error) {
    die("Connection failed/error: " . $dbconnection->connect_error);
}
```

echo "Connected successfully to database";
?>

phpMyAdmin

In case you do not want to rely on code to create and manage your databases, you can use the phpMyAdmin tool. Instead of relying on sending SQL queries, you will be given a user interface that is easier to use and reduces the chances of error since you do not need to type SQL and create typos. Think of it as Microsoft Access with a different interface.

The tool will also allow you to enter SQL if you want to and it will provide you with the SQL queries that it has used to perform the requests you make. Due to that, this tool will help you get more familiar with SQL. And the best thing about it is that it is free.

On the other hand, you can use phpMyAdmin to check the changes you made to the database while you are studying MySQL. If you do that, you will be able to debug faster since you do not need to redisplay or create a code for checking the contents of your database using PHP.

Conclusion

Thank you again for purchasing this book!

I hope this book was able to help you to master the fundamentals of MySQL programming.

The next step is to learn more about:

- Advanced SQL Statements and Clauses

- Attributes

- The MySQLi Class

- PHP Data Object

- Security Measures in MySQL

- Importing and Exporting MySQL Databases

- Different Applications of MySQL

Those topics will advance your MySQL programming skills. Well, even with the things you have learned here, you will already be capable of doing great things. With the knowledge you have, you can already create an online chat application, social network site, and online games!

That is no exaggeration. If you do not believe that, well, check out the sample codes that experts share on the web. You will be surprised how simple their codes are.

Finally, if you enjoyed this book, please take the time to share your thoughts and post a review on Amazon. We do our best to reach out to readers and provide the best value we can. Your positive review will help us achieve that. It'd be greatly appreciated!

Thank you and good luck!

Check Out My Other Books

Below you'll find some of my other popular books that are popular on Amazon and Kindle as well. Simply click on the links below to check them out. Alternatively, you can visit my author page on Amazon to see other work done by me.

Android Programming in a Day

Python Programming in a Day

C Programming Success in a Day

C Programming Professional Made Easy

JavaScript Programming Made Easy

PHP Programming Professional Made Easy

C ++ Programming Success in a Day

Windows 8 Tips for Beginners

HTML Professional Programming Made Easy

If the links do not work, for whatever reason, you can simply search for these titles on the Amazon website to find them.